The Library of American Choreographers™

JEROME ROBBINS

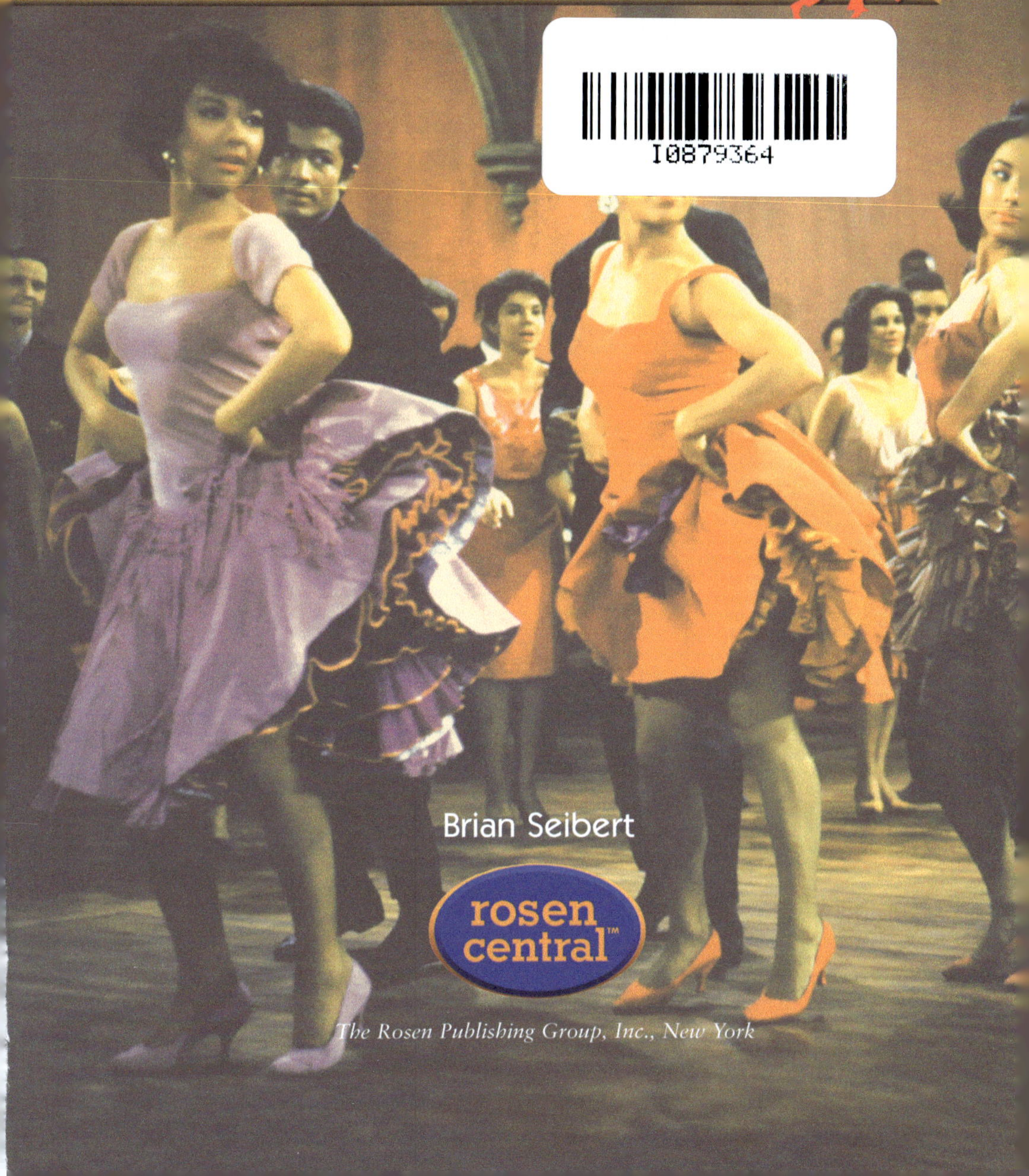

Brian Seibert

rosen central™

The Rosen Publishing Group, Inc., New York

In memory of Rick Sullivant

Published in 2006 by The Rosen Publishing Group, Inc.
29 East 21st Street, New York, NY 10010

First Edition

Library of Congress Cataloging-in-Publication Data

Seibert, Brian.
Jerome Robbins / Brian Seibert.— 1st ed.
p. cm.—(The library of American choreographers)
Includes bibliographical references and index.
ISBN 1-4042-0448-2 (lib. bdg.)
ISBN 1-4042-0642-6 (pbk. bdg.)
1. Robbins, Jerome—Juvenile literature. 2. Choreographers—United States—Biography—Juvenile literature.
I. Title. II. Series.
GV1785.R52S45 1996
792.8'2'092—dc22

2004030315

Manufactured in the United States of America

On the cover: A photo of Jerome Robbins in 1962. Background: The dance school scene from Robbins's *West Side Story*.

Contents

Introduction

At the start of the twentieth century, ballet barely existed in America. It was considered a European art form, and most people who performed ballet in the United States were foreigners.

The United States did, however, have a budding theatrical dance tradition of its own in the Broadway musical. The dancing in such shows was mostly limited to numbers featuring pretty but untrained chorus girls, and it usually had little to do with the story. By the 1930s, the situation was changing. A few Americans started organizing ballet companies of their own, and new choreographers for musical theater were emerging. Some of these choreographers had ballet training, but, in general, there was still almost no connection between ballet and Broadway.

That was before Jerome Robbins.

1 Early Life, Sudden Fame

The man who would become famous as Jerome Robbins was born in 1918 as Jerome Wilson Rabinowitz. Both of his parents were from Russia, and both were Jewish. Russia was not a very easy place for Jews to live at the time. Many Russians didn't like the way Jews had separate traditions and a different religion. At any moment, Jews could be spat upon, forced to leave their homes, or even killed. It was to escape such treatment that each of Robbins's parents moved to the United States around 1900. They had not known each other in Russia. Soon after meeting and marrying in New York City, they had a daughter, Sonia. Six years later, they had a son, Jerry.

As a child, Jerry was bursting with creativity. At age three, he started taking piano lessons, and it wasn't long before he was composing his own music and performing in recitals. He studied violin and painted. He wrote stories and poems. He was always

Jerome Robbins, seen here as a young dancer in a Spanish flamenco dance, would become famous for his many ballets and Broadway musicals that were inspired by cultures or times other than his own. He always did a lot of research on the dance, music, costumes, and customs of each place and period before he began his choreography.

acting out scenes from movies or entertaining his family with puppet shows.

His sister, Sonia, was a dancer. Jerry's first exposure to dance came while watching her practice and take classes. Sometimes, he joined in. When Sonia performed, magazine writers described her as a vision of loveliness. When she was old enough, Sonia moved out on her own and started a career as a dancer. This was a path that Jerry seemed unlikely to follow. The way his parents saw it, Jerry was a boy, and boys didn't dance.

Choosing a Career

Though Jerry's family owned a factory that made women's clothing, he wasn't interested in that kind of work. When he turned seventeen, he tried going to college, but he didn't like that either. He thought about becoming a journalist or a professional puppeteer, but he couldn't get a job in those fields. Sonia had an idea. She had always thought Jerry had talent as a dancer. She thought Jerry should audition for the Dance Center, an organization she performed with. She convinced their father to let Jerry try.

Senia Gluck Sandor, the director of the center, was impressed with Jerry's potential. "He had what you call a photographic memory," Sandor later told writer Emily Coleman. "Once he saw something, he could do it backward. Before I would do a thing, he had it." Sandor gave Jerry a scholarship and persuaded Jerry's parents to let him accept it.

Jerry later regretted not having finished college, but he always valued the education he gained at the Dance Center. Everything Sandor did inspired him. Jerry loved the way that Sandor's imagination could take something that seemed like an obstacle, such as the poles that held up the dance studio's ceiling, and make it part of a dance. Sandor asked his dancers to think like actors, imagining full lives for the characters they played—where they grew up, what they liked to eat. Jerry practiced this method the rest of his life.

At age eighteen, Jerry felt he had started late as a dancer, and he was eager to catch up. He took all kinds of classes, sometimes two a day—Spanish dance, Asian dances, choreography. Following Sandor's advice, he started studying ballet. In exchange for lessons, he cleaned the venetian blinds in the dance studio. To make money, he scrubbed floors and windows, pasted up posters, and ran errands.

During the summers, Jerry worked at Camp Tamiment in nearby Pennsylvania. Tamiment was a fun place, where talented young actors, singers, and dancers put on shows every week. Jerry thrived there. Audiences loved his theatrical flair. Tamiment's director let him try choreographing, not just for himself, but for an entire company of dancers. Jerry's choreography impressed everyone, and when the Tamiment group got the rare chance of performing on Broadway, Jerry's numbers were included in the show. Not many twenty-year-olds could call themselves Broadway choreographers.

Because of prejudice in America at the time, it was generally assumed that a Jewish name like Rabinowitz would hurt a performer's chances of success. So as Jerry started to appear in Broadway choruses and ballet concerts, he tried out a series of stage names—Robin Gerald, Gerald Robbins, Jerry Robyns. But it was as Jerome Robbins that he joined Ballet Theatre, one of the first ballet companies in the United States, shortly after it formed in 1940.

Dancing with Ballet Theatre

Robbins was a quick study. Playing small roles, he immediately drew attention to himself. Quickly, he gained a reputation as a vibrant, comic dancer, one with the timing necessary to make everyone laugh. Yet he was proudest of his portrayal of the sad puppet Petrouchka. He begged for a chance to have the part.

American Ballet Theatre

Ballet Theatre changed its name to American Ballet Theatre in 1957. The company still performs all over the world with a repertory that includes many Robbins ballets..

Created by the famous Russian choreographer Michel Fokine in 1911, Petrouchka is unattractive, friendless, and terribly different from everyone else. That was often how Robbins saw himself.

Ballet Theatre exposed Robbins to master choreographers. There was Fokine, who had been a great innovator forty years earlier. And there was the less-known but also brilliant Englishman Anthony Tudor, who used subtle gestures to express complicated emotions. Like Sandor, Tudor expected his dancers not just to dance his steps, but to know everything about the characters they played.

Robbins absorbed as much as he could from these men, dancing in their ballets and listening to their advice. He didn't wait long before proposing ballets of his own. For a while, Robbins had been noticing that many of Ballet Theatre's dances, such as Petrouchka, involved Russian folklore—too many, he thought. Why not

This photo shows Jerome Robbins as the sad puppet Petrouchka. This role was first danced by the great Russian ballet dancer Vaslav Nijinsky in 1911.

make a ballet based on an American theme? He didn't have to look far to find a good one. It was 1943, World War II was raging overseas, and the streets of New York were full of sailors on leave between battles. Robbins noticed that the sailors always traveled in threes, and he wrote up a story about what might happen if three of them could only find two girls as dates. When a slot suddenly opened up in the Ballet Theatre schedule, the company management decided to fill it with Robbins's short ballet. He had his chance.

First, Robbins had to find a composer. Someone suggested Leonard Bernstein, who was as young as Robbins and even more of a rising star. The two met, and Bernstein pulled out a napkin on which he had just written a tune. When he sang the melody, Robbins went crazy with joy. The music was exactly what the young choreographer had in mind—bold and jazzy, dreamy and a little sad.

On tour with Ballet Theatre, Robbins put together his new dance whenever he could. He would rehearse in hotel lobbies and trains, even while walking down the street. He cast his friends and based the characters on their personalities. One woman is sharp and experienced, the other more delicate and innocent. One sailor is a show-off; he spins in the air and lands in a split. Another is sweet and shy; he moves softly. The third sailor, the one Robbins played, is intense; he swings his hips and dances with an imaginary partner.

He called the ballet *Fancy Free*. It didn't look like most ballets that came before it, in which dancers wore tights and toe shoes. In *Fancy Free*, men in white sailor suits chase after women wearing high heels and skirts. They chew gum and fool around. As the story progresses, the three sailors compete for the attention of the two women in a bar. The men get in a fight, and the women leave. The sailors make up and become friends again, but when a third woman appears, they all rush after her. This was a situation you might have actually seen on the streets during World War II. A sharp observer, Robbins showed

Fancy Free, Robbins's first ballet, was a great success when it premiered in New York City in 1944. It was about contemporary American characters like the three sailors and young woman pictured here. This photo is from a performance of the original Ballet Theatre company at Covent Garden in London in 1946.

how funny and exciting it was—all through dance.

At its premiere in April 1944, *Fancy Free* received more than twenty curtain calls. Bernstein, Robbins, and the other dancers looked dazed as they took in the applause, shocked at their enormous success. The ballet became a big hit. It's still performed all over the world.

From *Fancy Free* to *On the Town*

Suddenly, all kinds of people became interested in what Robbins might do next. A friend convinced him and Bernstein to expand *Fancy Free* into the musical *On the Town*. This was a much more difficult challenge than creating a short ballet. Bernstein had never written a musical, and Robbins had only danced in the chorus of a few shows.

Fortunately, they found help in the experienced

director George Abbott. When Robbins choreographed a long ballet for the second act, Abbot split it in half, inserting a scene between the two parts. The director knew how to make a show fast and exciting. As always, Robbins listened and learned. Abbott became a mentor to him, and after *On the Town*, they worked together on five more shows.

By December of the same year, as the premiere of *On the Town* approached, Robbins was so nervous he disappeared entirely for two days. As it turned out, he had worried for nothing. Audiences loved the show. Many people thought that Robbins's dances were the best part.

Not much older than twenty-five, Robbins was already a success in two worlds—ballet and Broadway. It was around this time that he legally changed his name from Rabinowitz to Robbins. His parents, proud to be associated with their son, changed their names to Robbins, too.

2 Ballet Man, Broadway Man

For the rest of his life, Robbins would move back and forth between ballet and musical theater. Over the next ten years, he choreographed one musical comedy per year. And during almost every one of those years, he choreographed one or two ballets. For Robbins, ballet and musical theater were both satisfying but in different ways. With ballet, Robbins had more creative control, but musicals earned him much more money. At the time, most people working in ballet didn't think musical theater dancing was very serious, and people working in musical theater thought ballet was boring and stuffy. Robbins wouldn't let anyone tell him he had to choose one or the other. He needed the variety and liked how work in one realm spilled over into work in the other.

Although his second ballet, *Interplay* (1945), eventually became a part of the Ballet Theatre repertory, Robbins created it for a

Like Jerome Robbins, Leonard Bernstein (*pictured here*) worked in both classical and popular styles. In addition to his Broadway work, Bernstein was also well known as the conductor of the New York Philharmonic.

Broadway revue. *Interplay* resembles *Fancy Free* in many ways. The music is like jazz, the relaxed dancing mixes ballet steps with popular dance moves, and the dancers behave like contemporary teenagers—they play games like leapfrog, and they turn cartwheels. While *Interplay* doesn't follow a narrative or story, what holds the audience's interest is how Robbins has arranged the dancers into fascinating patterns, and the way he has them dance for each other in a friendly competition that no one wins. Robbins and his dancers worked hard in order to create the illusion that they were making up everything on the spot.

Facsimile (1946), the next ballet Robbins created, was totally different. Once again, the music was composed by Bernstein, but where *Fancy Free* and

Interplay were lighthearted, this new ballet expressed intense feelings of fear and loneliness. The story follows three adults who hide their insecurity in fake politeness. Robbins wanted to explore serious themes.

Making Broadway Laugh

There was little chance for him to pursue those themes on Broadway. Musical producers were more interested in his comic gifts. His next musical, *Billion Dollar Baby* (1945), was set in the 1920s. Robbins intensively researched the period. He pored over cartoons and films to discover how people in the twenties dressed and acted. One memorable number featured the Charleston, the era's most popular dance. Using an approach that was unusual among Broadway choreographers, Robbins gave each member of the chorus a recognizable character to play—a policeman, for example, a shy girl, or a stuck-up snob. They all danced the Charleston in inventive and funny ways, kicking up their legs until they collapsed.

A similar level of research went into his work for *High Button Shoes* (1947), set in 1913. The highlight of the show is a hilarious chase scene Robbins based on silent film comedies. Pursuing a bag of money, the characters go in and out of a row of bathhouses. A bathing beauty goes in one door, but a crook comes out of it. A few seconds later, a cop follows—all from the same door. Later, a whole family of crooks stream out of one door while a gorilla pops out of another. The craziness seems likely to spin out of control, but it was all carefully designed by Robbins.

His work for *High Button Shoes* earned Robbins the first of many Tony Awards for choreography. But being a successful choreographer wasn't enough for him; he wanted to direct. For his next musical, *Look Ma I'm Dancin'* (1948), he shared the role of director with his old mentor George Abbott. He also wrote the story—and in a sense, he lived it. The plot was very similar to his own experiences with Ballet Theatre, especially the role of a young dancer-choreographer obsessed with success.

When Robbins was offered the chance to direct a musical himself, he took it. The show was called *That's the Ticket* (1948), and it marked his first flop. Looking back later, he took the blame for the failure; he hadn't been ready. The disappointment Robbins felt might partially explain the enormous, life-changing decision he made next.

Joining Balanchine

That year, 1948, the New York City Ballet (NYCB) presented its first season.

Robbins saw a performance and was amazed. The choreographer, George Balanchine, was fourteen years older than Robbins. After receiving the best ballet training possible in his boyhood home of Russia, Balanchine had already been successful as a choreographer in Europe. Robbins had danced for him in two musicals, but it was at the 1948 performance that Robbins realized what the rest of the world would soon acknowledge: Balanchine was the greatest ballet choreographer of his day.

Robbins wrote a letter asking if there was any way he could help the new company. In response, he received an invitation to join the New York City Ballet as a dancer and choreographer. He would never return to Ballet Theatre. At NYCB, Robbins continued to excel as a dancer. Balanchine cast him in new

New York City Ballet

The New York City Ballet began to form in 1933, when a rich, well-educated young man named Lincoln Kirstein invited George Balanchine to come to America and start a school. It took fifteen more years to develop the dancers and raise the money necessary to found a permanent company.

George Balanchine (1904–1983) and Jerome Robbins lead the New York City Ballet in a rehearsal of the version of the ballet *Pulcinella* that they choreographed together. Born in Russia, Balanchine moved to the United States in 1933 to create the first American ballet company. Robbins greatly admired Balanchine and was honored to be the associate director of his company.

ballets and revived an important early work to show off his dramatic gift. Robbins danced in his own ballets, too, but it was as a choreographer that he flourished. Balanchine believed in Robbins's talent and encouraged him to undertake more choreography.

Over the next seven years, Robbins created nine ballets and one more in collaboration with Balanchine. He retired from dancing in 1952, but he was nowhere near retirement as a choreographer. Always keeping a foot in the musical theater world, he gained a reputation as a reliable "doctor," someone who could be called in to fix shows that weren't working. During the same seven years, he doctored at least four shows and served as choreographer for seven more.

The King and I

Some of his best choreography was for *The King and I* (1951). The composer and lyricist, Richard Rodgers and Oscar Hammerstein II, were then the most successful creative team on Broadway. Set in the 1860s, the story follows a widowed Englishwoman named Anna to what is now Thailand, where she teaches the children of the king.

As usual, Robbins thoroughly researched his subject. He studied books and figurative Thai sculpture and sought the advice of Asian dancers. The dances he created were more than delightful; they helped tell the story. During "Getting to Know You," Anna and an Asian dancer try to bridge the cultural divide by mimicking each other's movements. The Asian dancer wears a traditional pajama-like outfit, while Anna wears a hoopskirt that shoots out from her hips like a big umbrella. In Robbins's clever choreography, four women gather around the Asian dancer's legs as if they were her hoopskirt. Later, Anna and the king fall in love but are too prideful to admit it. In "Shall We Dance," Robbins has the pair express their love by spinning around the room, dancing a polka in each other's arms.

The number that gained the most attention was "The Small House of Uncle Thomas," a short ballet performed by the king's wives and slaves. The ballet's story comes from *Uncle Tom's Cabin*, a book written by Harriet Beecher Stowe in 1853 to criticize American slavery. Narrated by one of the king's slaves, the ballet serves as a subtle criticism of the king's own practice of slavery.

In the dance, a slave woman and her baby try to escape their master. Robbins's choreography captures the poetry and the danger of the situation and makes creative use of Asian dance traditions. The woman hops on one foot, determined but frail. Dancers in dog masks, at once scary and funny, pursue the woman, lifting their hind legs in the air. The woman and her baby come to a river, represented by rippling fabric. When a god makes the river freeze and they can make it across, the cloth is pulled tight. The woman and an angel skate on the ice together.

This photo shows a scene from the Asian-inspired ballet "The Small House of Uncle Thomas," which is part of the Broadway production *The King and I*. Robbins directed and choreographed the show in 1951. Like many of Robbins's Broadway shows, *The King and I* was so popular that it was revived many times. This photo is from the 1989 revival.

The King and I was very popular. Demand was high enough, in fact, to keep the show running for 1,246 performances. Five years later, even larger audiences were charmed by a movie version that kept Robbins's choreography mostly intact.

Something to Fear

The next ballet Robbins created for NYCB certainly wasn't charming. In *The Cage* (1951), Robbins presented a colony of female insects that kill any males who enter their midst. One young insect proves herself to the rest by snapping a man's neck with her legs. She tries to protect the next man—she likes him, and they dance sweetly together—but the other insects force her to kill him, too. The way Robbins twisted traditional ballet movements made the dance terrifying; the sweet parts made it sad.

Charming or not, *The Cage* was received well. Right after the premiere, however, Robbins left for Europe, where he stayed for months. Paramount Pictures offered him a six-year movie contract, but he turned it down. For a man who seemed to have everything going for him, Robbins was acting strangely, as though he were afraid of something.

He had reason to be. Suspicion was spreading through the United States like a contagious disease. The country's chief enemy, the Soviet Union, had recently developed an atom bomb, and people feared a takeover by secret Soviet agents. Congress set up committees to investigate the possibility. The House Un-American Activities Committee (HUAC) was particularly interested in the influence of Hollywood and Broadway (especially artists like Robbins) on the viewing public. Newspaper articles

Jerome Robbins takes an oath at the hearings of the House Un-American Activities Committee. Robbins's testimony was met with much controversy from the artistic community.

suggested that the committee should question him.

Artists associated with the Communist Party were prevented from working. Politicians were taking advantage of the fear of Communism and exerting power over anyone who criticized the government. The lives of many good people who resisted the bullying were ruined. Some went to jail; others committed suicide.

When Robbins was called before the committee, he admitted that he had joined the Communist Party in 1943. Like many, he had been attracted to the party because it claimed to be committed to justice for minorities such as Jews. Robbins testified that joining the party had been a mistake and that he had cut his ties to the organization. Then he gave the committee the names of people he knew who had also belonged to the party.

Even though Robbins knew he was creating serious problems for the people whose names he gave, he did it anyway. He feared that if he didn't give the names, his career would be ruined. Many people, including some of Robbins's closest friends, never forgave him for handing over those names. Robbins never forgave himself.

3 Choreographer-Director

Robbins responded to his painful encounter with the House Un-American Activities Committee the way he reacted to most difficult episodes in his life: he got back to work. In particular, he picked up his dream of becoming a director.

Peter Pan (1954), Robbins's first successful directing project, was based on J. M. Barrie's beloved children's story about a boy who refuses to grow up. It was a perfect match for Robbins's lifelong ability to capture the spirit of youth. As the actress who played Peter later pointed out, Robbins *was* Peter Pan. He created funny dances to make the villains less scary, and he sent the cast flying through the air on hidden strings. As a director, he dusted the entire show with a gentle comedy that appealed to children and grown-ups alike.

Robbins got the chance to direct again with the musical *Bells Are Ringing* (1956). An even bigger triumph came the following year. *West Side Story* (1957) is probably the show for which Robbins is most famous, and it took a long struggle to put it together. In 1949, Robbins had suggested to his friend Leonard Bernstein and the playwright Arthur Laurents that they update the story of *Romeo and Juliet*. But almost ten years passed before they all decided to retell Shakespeare's story as a conflict between gangs in modern-day New York.

Robbins, Bernstein, Laurents, and the young lyricist Stephen Sondheim attempted to apply their experience in ballet, classical music, and serious drama to musical theater. The style they came up with for the musical was new—more poetic, like a ballet. As choreographer and director, Robbins blurred the line between dance and drama, giving choreography a greater role in defining character and telling the story.

West Side Story

In the beginning of the show, the gang members don't speak or sing. Instead, Robbins expresses how they live by how they move. Crouching over and snapping their fingers, they prowl the city streets in packs, full of energy yet desperate to look cool. Their sudden bursts of movement—arms shooting in all directions—show how short-tempered they are, how nervous. Later, when the doomed lovers Maria and Tony first meet, Robbins shows that the shy couple is falling in love by having them slowly dance together. They stare into each other's eyes but don't touch.

As a director, Robbins pushed his performers to become their characters. He called the actors by their character names and insisted they use those names with each other, even outside rehearsal. Members of one gang were not allowed to talk with members of the other, even during lunch breaks. Staging a dance competition between the two gangs, Robbins rehearsed the groups separately, so that when they finally danced together, each group was genuinely surprised by what the other group did.

Robbins expected nothing less than perfection, and he constantly pushed his cast—and himself—toward that impossible goal. He also had a nasty temper, and if things weren't going well, he would often take it out on one of the performers. This was true of him throughout his life. Outside of rehearsals, he was funny and fun to be with. But when the pressure was on, he could become cruel. He fought with his collaborators all the time. Ultimately, people put up with his behavior only because he was so talented.

West Side Story was a hit, and when the movie

This photo is from the movie version of *West Side Story*. Robbins's choreography captured the emotional energy of real gangs on the west side of Manhattan. The crouching posture and tightly enclosed grouping of these dancers reflect the gang members' character and relationship.

was made a few years later, Robbins was asked to codirect. Although his mind buzzed with innovative filmmaking ideas, he had trouble adapting to the ways of Hollywood. In his search for perfection, he shot scenes over and over, quickly eating up the budget. Eventually, he was fired and the film was finished without him. Robbins remained bitter about the experience for the rest of his life.

More Ballets and a Company of His Own

Robbins always had less trouble in the world of ballet. In the years that he was working on *Peter Pan* and *West Side Story*, Robbins created two very different masterpieces at NYCB. *Afternoon of a Faun* was originally choreographed in 1912 by the famous Russian dancer Vaslav Nijinsky. Nijinsky's version, set to the music of French composer Claude Debussy, tells a story about a faun—a character from Greek mythology. Robbins's 1953 ballet is set to the same music, of Claude Debussy, but it is about dancers, one of Robbins's favorite subjects. A shirtless young man sleeping on the floor of a rehearsal studio wakes, looking in the direction of the audience as if it were a mirror. A young woman in pointe shoes comes in to practice, and the two dance together, watching themselves in the "mirror" as they try out moves. When the man kisses the woman's cheek, the mood shifts, but after she looks at him and touches the spot where he kissed her, she leaves, and the man stretches out on the floor once again.

Where *Afternoon of a Faun* created a mysterious poetry out of dancers' behaviors, *The Concert* (1956) used the music of Frédéric Chopin to make a hundred jokes. One section

Jerome Robbins (*right*) is seen here working with New York City Ballet dancers on his comic ballet, *The Concert*. This piece, set to the music of Chopin, is a humorous look at all the things that can go wrong during a ballet performance.

shows a group of ballerinas who clearly haven't rehearsed enough. They try to dance together but continually make mistakes. One ballerina goes to the right while the rest move left; another puts her arms above her head while everyone else's stay by their waists. A wonder of comic timing, *The Concert* is probably one of the funniest ballets ever made.

In 1958, Robbins started his own company called Ballets: USA. The government that had once accused him of being un-American now sent him and his young dancers on a tour of Europe, exhibiting them as representatives of the best that the United States had to offer. Finding them new and exciting, Europeans enthusiastically welcomed the group. One critic in London called the company "the greatest thing in ballet for twenty years."

All the works performed by Ballets: USA were choreographed by Robbins. The dancers in *New York Export: Opus Jazz* (1958) are reminiscent of the gang members in *West Side Story*. Wearing sneakers and snapping their fingers, they move in packs and show off for each other. The stage patterns in *Opus Jazz*, however, are much more complex and the overall feeling of the piece is much darker. At one point, three men toss a woman around roughly, then throw her offstage. In another dance, *Moves* (1959), there's no music at all, and the choreography is even more complicated and bleak.

When the government sponsorship ended in 1961, so did Ballets: USA. The demise of the company didn't make Robbins any less busy. A proven director of musicals, he

From Robbins's Program Note for Ballets: USA

"I believe very strongly that ballet dancing in America, originally an imported product . . . has been completely influenced and drastically changed by the culture in which it has grown up. We in America dress, eat, think, talk and walk differently from any other people. We also dance differently."

was in demand on Broadway. *Gypsy* (1959) tells the true-life story of a mother who tries to turn her daughters into vaudeville stars.

Gypsy was praised by critics and was popular with the public, but it wasn't Robbins's favorite show. Robbins agreed with many people that *Gypsy*'s story was more important than its dancing, and he was tired of sharing control with collaborators and producers he might disagree with. He talked of starting a theater of his own. He also wanted more credit. In all the advertisements and programs for *Gypsy*, he insisted that his name be printed separately from the others. And to make clear which person was most important, he wanted his name outlined by a box.

A Family Musical

Throughout his career, Robbins often had trouble committing to new projects. Frequently, he would agree to join a production, change his mind and quit, then return later to work his "doctoring" magic. The decision to direct *Fiddler on the Roof* (1964), though, was easy. The musical focuses on the life of poor Jews in Russia, the life his parents had left behind. Directing *Fiddler* was a way to embrace part of himself he had long resisted.

Robbins's preparations for the show were as thorough as ever, only this time he was studying his own heritage. He brought all of his skills to the project. In rehearsals, he created acting exercises to help the cast understand what it felt like to be a member of a hated minority. And once he discovered that the show was about tradition, he made sure that every moment in the musical related to the theme, including his choreography. Robbins designed his dances to occur naturally, as they might in life.

Even so, some dancing stood out, such as the moment at a wedding when a man balancing a bottle on his head begins to spin slowly. Soon another man joins hands with him, balancing a bottle on his own head. Then two more join, also with bottles, and, incredibly, they all slowly kneel. Arms locked together, they thrust out their legs, again and again, never dropping the bottles. The feat is thrilling, but the moment—like the image in the show's title—also expresses something more: the Jewish spirit of survival.

Fiddler won award after award. It became the longest-running musical in Broadway history, was performed around the world, and made Robbins a rich man. His greatest moment of triumph, however, may have come earlier, on opening night, when he looked into his father's eyes and saw tears of joy.

4 Later Life and Legacy

Fiddler was Robbins's last original Broadway musical. For the rest of his life, he seldom strayed from his other realm—the world of ballet. There he didn't have to share control, and the only limits were his own and those of his dancers.

In 1966, still dreaming of combining ballet and theater, he founded an experimental workshop called the American Theatre Laboratory. As he explained later to Deborah Jowitt in *New York Magazine*, what he was searching for was an escape from the financial pressures of Broadway. He wanted "the kind of freedom you have in the ballet studio when you are creating. Unknown things come out of you."

The American Theatre Laboratory never staged any productions, but the experience seemed to give Robbins new life. In 1969, when he returned to the New York City Ballet after ten years, it was as if a dam had broken. His enormous energy concentrated in one direction, Robbins began to create ballet after ballet—twenty in the decade that followed.

The first was *Dances at a Gathering* (1969), a joyful, hour-long work overflowing with choreographic invention. Without telling a story, the ballet manages to celebrate love and youth. Mixing folk gestures with classical ballet steps, Robbins makes both kinds of movement look equally natural. Almost everyone who saw the ballet loved it, including Robbins's hero, George Balanchine. After the first performance, Balanchine found the younger choreographer backstage and gave him a kiss on each cheek—Russian style.

Staying with Ballet, Still Searching

Robbins was always setting himself challenges. His ballets grew longer, as if he were trying to test the attention span of NYCB audiences. *The Goldberg Variations* (1971), set to very complicated music by J. S. Bach, clocks in at one hour and twenty minutes. While many people at the time thought it was too long, others admired how the ballet matched the complexity of the music.

Watermill (1972) is almost as long as *The Goldberg Variations*, but where one is filled with activity, barely anything happens in the other. Influenced by Japanese theater, *Watermill* moves so slowly that time seems to stop. Even more so than was the case for *The Goldberg Variations*, the response to *Watermill* was mixed. Many people thought it was beautiful. Others booed.

More and more, Robbins avoided the gift for storytelling that had made him famous. In 1974, he teamed up with Bernstein again to create *Dybbuk*, a ballet based on a Jewish play about demons. Instead of telling the story, Robbins made a series of related dances evoking the mood of dark magic. The ballet was barely finished before Robbins started cutting it. He took out even more of the story and renamed it *Dybbuk Variations*. Later, he reduced it even further, calling it *A Suite of Dances* (1980).

Robbins hadn't entirely lost his sense of fun, though. In *Circus Polka* (1972), he himself took the stage as a ringmaster, playfully cracking his whip as he directed a troupe of children lined up in order of descending size—little, littler, littlest. And when creating *Ma Mère l'Oye* (*Mother Goose*) (1975), Robbins once again let loose his theatrical magic to show a group of young dancers gathering whatever props they can find to act out fairy tales.

Jerome Robbins cracks the whip over students from the School of American Ballet in his ballet *Circus Polka*. The School of American Ballet is the official school of the New York City Ballet.

Looking toward the future, Robbins kept up with the trends in experimental dance and music and incorporated many of the new approaches in his later ballets. Looking toward the past, he created ballets based on the old-fashioned elegance of Fred Astaire and images from ancient Greek sculpture.

Securing His Legacy

Some of Robbins's later works focus on death and loss. Balanchine, the choreographer he admired

A Generous Man

Robbins donated a percentage of his earnings from *Fiddler on the Roof* to the Dance Collection of the New York Public Library of the Performing Arts. Over the years, that sum grew into millions of dollars, helping make the collection the largest in the world. The library named its film and video archive after Robbins in gratitude.

most and who was his chief role model for more than thirty years, died in 1983. As Robbins grew into his seventies, he became concerned about his own legacy—about what would happen to his work after he died.

Many of his ballets had been filmed and documented by Labanotation, a symbol system for recording movement, but most of his theater work had not. Robbins decided to re-create some of his Broadway dances for filming, but the project quickly snowballed. Before long, he had envisioned an enormous Broadway show composed of reconstructed highlights from his entire career. It was called *Jerome Robbins' Broadway* (1989).

Robbins had great fun applying his research skills to reconstructing his own work. He hunted down any remaining evidence—from newspaper photos to amateur film footage—and searched the memories of all living participants. Amid all the reminiscing, it became clear that Robbins's work habits hadn't eased with age. He drove his cast hard, rehearsing them ten hours a day for six months—a period two or three times longer than standard Broadway practice. He felt his legacy was on the line.

The work paid off. *Jerome Robbins' Broadway* won Robbins his fifth Tony Award. Critics marveled at how the numbers from the past hadn't lost the power to entertain. In terms of craftsmanship and imagination, they said, Robbins's old routines were far better than anything else on Broadway in the late 1980s.

In 1990, Robbins officially retired from the New York City Ballet. The company honored him by putting on a festival featuring twenty-eight of his ballets. All of the dancers joined him on the stage as he took a final bow.

Nonetheless, Robbins wasn't quite done choreographing. In 1994, he created another Bach ballet, and the following year, he made a crowd-pleasing suite of his dances from *West Side Story*. In 1997, he finished yet another ballet to the music of Bach. Called *Brandenburg*, it was Robbins's sixty-sixth ballet, and it would be his last. He died of a stroke on

Jerome Robbins accepts a prestigious Tony Award in 1989. Robbins won for the Broadway show *Jerome Robbins' Broadway*. During his long career, he won six Tony Awards, including Best Musical and Best Director.

The great dance critic Edwin Denby once described Robbins as "the most gifted of American-born ballet choreographers." Denby made the comment in 1947, but when Robbins died fifty-one years later, it remained true.

Denby also noted that Robbins's originality lay less in the steps he created than in the spirit with which they were danced—fresh, sincere, and spontaneous. Along with Balanchine, Robbins made classical ballet American, adapting the European technique and tradition to American rhythms and themes, incorporating native gestures and attitudes. And perhaps even more than his mentor Balanchine, Robbins reshaped the art with an American imagination.

That would have been achievement enough, but Robbins also remade the American musical, using dance to tell the story, making movement as important as music and spoken scenes. Other choreographers had pioneered this development. In 1936, Balanchine had stitched a ballet into the story of the musical *On Your Toes*. And in 1943, Agnes de Mille had pushed the idea further in *Oklahoma!* But Robbins went the furthest in weaving dance, story, and music into a single fabric.

After Robbins came a line of choreographer-directors that dominated Broadway for decades—Bob Fosse, Gower Cham- pion, Michael Bennett, and others. Robbins served as mentor to many and an example to all, but none of those choreographer-directors ever matched Robbins's range or the depth of his artistry. And none of them made great ballets. Robbins's double achievement is unsurpassed.

Glossary

bathhouse A building with dressing rooms for swimmers.

Charleston A fast ballroom dance popular in the 1920s.

choreographer A person who creates or arranges dances and ballets.

choreography The art of creating or arranging dances and ballets.

company A group of dancers.

critic A professional who analyzes and evaluates works of art, such as ballet performances.

curtain calls The appearance of performers or a performer at the end of a performance in response to applause.

legacy Something handed down from the past.

mentor A trusted teacher.

number One of the separate offerings in a program of entertainment.

pointe shoes Stiffened shoes that support a dancer's foot to allow dancing on one's toes.

polka A lively dance from Eastern Europe performed by couples.

rehearse To practice in preparation for a performance.

repertory The collection of works a dance company knows and can perform.

revive To bring back to life or restore to use.

revue A musical show consisting of short, varied songs and dances.

season A series of regularly scheduled performances.

stage name The name by which a performer is known to the public.

suite A group of related things intended to be used together. Also a musical work made up of a series of sections, usually for dance.

toe shoes Same as "pointe shoes."

Tony Awards The annual awards for outstanding achievement in the theater.

tour A journey to perform in different places.

vaudeville Stage entertainment that was popular in the early twentieth century. It offered a variety of short acts, including performances by singers, dancers, comedians, jugglers, acrobats, and trained animals.

For More Information

Web Sites

Due to the changing nature of Internet links, the Rosen Publishing Group, Inc., has developed an online list of Web sites related to the subject of this book. This site is updated regularly. Please use this link to access the list:

http://www.rosenlinks.com/lac/jero

For Further Reading

Feldman, Jane, and Eva Leiman. *I Am a Dancer*. New York, NY: Random House Children's Books, 1999.

Greskovic, Robert. *Ballet 101: A Complete Guide to Learning and Loving the Ballet.* New York, NY: Hyperion, 1998.

Bibliography

Burton, William Westbrook, ed. *Conversations About Bernstein*. London, England: Oxford University Press, 1995.

Coleman, Emily. "From Tutus to T-Shirts." *New York Magazine*, October 8, 1961, pp. 30, 32.

Conrad, Christine. *Jerome Robbins: That Broadway Man, That Ballet Man*. London, England: Booth-Clibborn Editions, 2000.

Croce, Arlene. *Writing in the Dark*. New York, NY: Farrar, Straus and Giroux, 2000.

Denby, Edwin. *Dance Writings and Poetry*. New Haven, CT: Yale University Press, 1998.

Jowitt, Deborah. "Back Again to Ballet." *New York Magazine*, December 8, 1974, pp. II, 45.

Jowitt, Deborah. *Jerome Robbins: His Life, His Theater, His Dance*. New York, NY: Simon and Schuster, 2004.

Long, Robert Emmet. *Broadway, the Golden Years: Jerome Robbins and the Great Choreographer-Directors 1940 to the Present*. New York, NY: Continuum, 2002.

Reynolds, Nancy, and Malcolm McCormick. *No Fixed Points: Dance in the Twentieth Century*. New Haven, CT: Yale University

Index

About the Author

Brian Seibert has written about dance for the *Village Voice*, the *New Yorker*, and the *New York Times*. He started studying dance at age six because he was terrible at soccer and his mother thought dance classes might make him more coordinated. He never returned to soccer.

Photo Credits

Cover, p. 25 © Bettmann/Corbis; cover (background), p. 1 © Ernst Haas/Getty Images; p. 6 photograph by Maurice Seymour, courtesy of Ronald Seymour; pp. 11, 20, 32, 39 © Jerome Robbins Dance Division, the New York Public Library for the Performing Arts, Astor, Lenox, and Tilden Foundations; p. 13 © Baron/Getty Images; p. 16 © CSU Archives, courtesy Everett Collection; pp. 20, 39 © Martha Swope; p. 23 © Henry Grossman/Time Life Pictures/Getty Images; p. 30 © courtesy Everett Collection; p. 42 © AP/Wide World Photos.

Designer: Tahara Anderson
Developmental Editor: Nancy Allison, CMA, RME